FORGOTTEN FACTS ABOUT LIFE DURING THE AMERICAN REVOLUTION

BY KATHLEEN CONNORS

HISTORY'S FORGOTTEN FACTS

Enslow PUBLISHING

Please visit our website, www.enslow.com. For a free color catalog of all our high-quality books, call toll free 1-800-398-2504 or fax 1-877-980-4454.

Library of Congress Cataloging-in-Publication Data
Names: Connors, Kathleen, author.
Title: Forgotten facts about life during the American Revolution / Kathleen Connors.
Description: Buffalo, New York : Enslow Publishing, 2024. | Series: History's forgotten facts | Includes index. | Audience: Grades 2-3
Identifiers: LCCN 2023026632 (print) | LCCN 2023026633 (ebook) | ISBN 9781978537675 (library binding) | ISBN 9781978537668 (paperback) | ISBN 9781978537682 (ebook)
Subjects: LCSH: United States–History–Revolution, 1775-1783–Juvenile literature.
Classification: LCC E208 .C685 2024 (print) | LCC E208 (ebook) | DDC 973.3–dc23/eng/20230607
LC record available at https://lccn.loc.gov/2023026632
LC ebook record available at https://lccn.loc.gov/2023026633

Published in 2024 by
Enslow Publishing
2544 Clinton Street
Buffalo, NY 14224

Portions of this work were originally authored by Kristen Rajczak and published as *Life During the American Revolution*. All new material in this edition authored by Kathleen Connors.

Designer: Tanya Dellaccio Keeney
Editor: Kristen Rajczak Nelson

Photo credits: Cover, series background (banners) Ledelena/Shutterstock.com; cover, series background (paper) Vitaly Korovin/Shutterstock.com; cover, series background (wood) Pataradon Luangtongkum/Shutterstock.com; cover (main image) traveler1116/iStock.com; p. 5 https://upload.wikimedia.org/wikipedia/commons/3/3b/The_Battle_of_Lexington.jpg; p. 7 https://upload.wikimedia.org/wikipedia/commons/c/cb/A_New_Method_of_Maracrony_Making_as_Practised_at_Boston_in_North_America_MET_MM2283.jpg; pp. 8, 9 Courtesy of the New York Public Library; p. 10 https://upload.wikimedia.org/wikipedia/commons/9/9f/BattleofMonmouth.jpg; pp. 11, 13 (bottom), 19 Courtesy of the Library of Congress; p. 13 (top) https://upload.wikimedia.org/wikipedia/commons/e/eb/Infantry%2C_Continental_Army%2C_1779-1783.jpg; p. 15 Anadolu_Dizgi/Shutterstock.com; p. 17 https://upload.wikimedia.org/wikipedia/commons/0/01/Spinninginthecolonialkitchen.jpg.

Printed in the United States of America

CPSIA compliance information: Batch #CWENS24: For further information contact Enslow Publishing at 1-800-398-2504.

CONTENTS

Words in the glossary appear in **bold** type the first time they are used in the text.

FAR FROM UNITED

By the 1760s, many people in the 13 British **colonies** in North America were unhappy. The king of England would not listen to their concerns. Colonists had no say in their own laws. In 1775, the fight for independence began.

We look back at the American **Revolution** and think of the heroes who fought for freedom. But more than 2 million colonists lived in America by the mid-1770s—and not all of them wanted a revolution!

COLONISTS WHO BACKED THE REVOLUTION CALLED THEMSELVES **PATRIOTS**. HOWEVER, THE BRITISH SAW THEM AS **REBELS**.

DON'T FORGET!

The American Revolution began on April 19, 1775, with the Battles of Lexington and Concord in Massachusetts.

STAYING LOYAL

While the patriots' call for revolution was loud enough to spark a war, they weren't in the majority. Many colonists didn't know which side to **support**. They tried to stay out of the war.

Historians say about 20 percent of colonists wanted to stay a part of the British kingdom. These colonists were called Loyalists or Tories. Some joined British forces to fight the patriots—who could be their neighbors or family members!

DON'T FORGET!

Sometimes, Loyalists who voiced their support for the British were publicly covered in tar and feathers!

THE PATRIOTS CONSIDERED LOYALISTS TO BE **TRAITORS**. STORIES OF POOR TREATMENT, INCLUDING TARRING AND FEATHERING, CAUSED MANY LOYALISTS TO RUN AWAY TO CANADA OR BACK TO GREAT BRITAIN.

LEADERS REMEMBERED

The leaders of the American Revolution, including Paul Revere, George Washington, and Samuel Adams, are names we still remember today. Streets and buildings are named for them. Cities have put up statues in their honor.

THE BATTLE OF BUNKER HILL

DON'T FORGET!

There were spies, or secret scouts, during the American Revolution! Men—and sometimes women—went behind British lines to find out their plans.

STARK WAS JUST ONE OF MANY PATRIOTS WHO FOUGHT FOR FREEDOM BUT HASN'T REALLY BEEN REMEMBERED IN HISTORY CLASSES.

Some patriots' efforts aren't as well known. Do you know John Stark? Once Stark heard about the first shots of the war, he gathered 400 men. He marched them to Boston, Massachusetts. His group helped the patriots in the Battle of Bunker Hill!

MILITIAMEN

The main fighting force of the colonies against Great Britain was the Continental army, led by George Washington. At times during the revolution, colonial militias supported the army. These small fighting forces **defended** the colony's borders.

DON'T FORGET!

Instead of joining the Continental army, most men chose to be part of a militia. They mostly fought near their homes and were able to choose their own leaders.

GEORGE WASHINGTON DIDN'T RESPECT MILITIAMEN. HE WROTE THAT "TO PLACE ANY **DEPENDENCE** UPON MILITIA IS ASSUREDLY RESTING UPON A BROKEN STAFF."

The extra men militias provided weren't always helpful. They were poorly **organized** and poorly trained. In farming communities, militiamen would leave the battlefield when it was time to bring in their crops! In addition, the British army easily overcame the militias.

JOIN UP!

The soldiers in the Continental army weren't all big supporters of the revolution. In fact, many were forced or paid to sign up. Washington found the men who willingly signed up weren't good soldiers to start. They joined because they had few skills to bring them better opportunities.

Furthermore, the army struggled with little food, poor housing, and a limited amount of clothing. Some soldiers didn't have shoes. There weren't even enough guns for men in battle!

PATRIOT SOLDIERS OFTEN WORE COATS OR SHIRTS OF DARK BLUE OR BROWN. THROUGH THE THICK SMOKE OF BATTLE, A MAN'S COAT WAS OFTEN ALL SOLDIERS COULD USE TO TELL WHO THE ENEMY WAS.

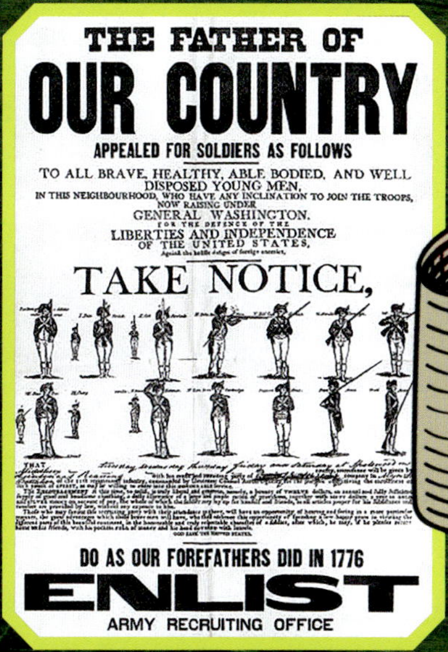

DON'T FORGET!

The Continental army never had enough men. Washington always wanted the army to be much larger.

BATTLES AND BEYOND

From the Battle of Trenton to the **Siege** of Yorktown, the battles of the American Revolution could be bloody. Some happened right on a farmer's land or in a town square!

But not all the fighting happened out in the open. Patriot soldiers would shoot at the British army from behind walls. They would crawl on their bellies to hide before attacking. The British soldiers weren't used to this kind of fighting, and it often worked!

DON'T FORGET!

The British army, like the colonists, were divided. Some believed their job was to win over the rebels and bring them back into the British empire, or kingdom. Some wanted to use any means necessary to stop the rebels.

THIS MAP SHOWS WHERE SOME OF THE MAJOR BATTLES OF THE AMERICAN REVOLUTION OCCURRED.

LIFE GOES ON?

It was hard to ignore the American Revolution as it went on. Many fathers and brothers were off fighting in the war. Both armies took food and supplies from homes near their camps.

But colonists did the best they could to continue with everyday life. Shops sold goods, and families worked their farmland. Women stepped into roles the men left behind. In addition to cooking, cleaning, and taking care of children, women ran their husband's businesses and worked in the fields.

MANY WOMEN ALSO HAD TO STAND UP TO FORCEFUL SOLDIERS FROM BOTH ARMIES AND GUARD THEIR LAND.

DON'T FORGET!

In colonial society, women weren't equal to men. Men owned the family land and were the head of their household.

WOMEN AT WAR

Not all women stayed home during the American Revolution! Some traveled with the British or patriot forces. Many of these women, called camp followers, were soldiers' wives. They washed clothing, cooked, and helped care for the sick and wounded.

Some camp followers learned to fire cannons—just in case they were ever needed. One of these women, Margaret Corbin, put her knowledge to use in 1776 when her husband was killed while using a cannon.

DEBORAH SAMPSON DRESSED AS A MAN IN ORDER TO JOIN THE CONTINENTAL ARMY! THE ARMY DIDN'T DISCOVER HER SECRET FOR A YEAR AND A HALF.

DEBORAH SAMPSON

DON'T FORGET!

If the British captured a **regiment**, the camp followers were captured too!

FREEDOM FOR ALL?

When the American Revolution ended in 1783, the 13 colonies were free of British rule. Still, not everyone who lived there was free. By the 1770s, more than 400,000 enslaved people lived in the colonies.

Some earned their freedom by joining the British army or serving in the place of their enslaver in the Continental army. However, most didn't fight in the war. Freedom for all Americans didn't come until more than 80 years later!

DON'T FORGET!

Southern states didn't want enslaved people fighting in the army. They feared rebellions if too many were armed.

THE BRITISH SURRENDERED A LARGE PART OF THEIR ARMY AT YORKTOWN. THERE WAS NO HOPE FOR THEM TO WIN THE WAR AFTER THAT.

DATES TO REMEMBER

APRIL 19, 1775

THE BATTLES OF LEXINGTON AND CONCORD START THE WAR.

JULY 1776

THE DECLARATION OF INDEPENDENCE IS ADOPTED.

DECEMBER 26, 1776

WASHINGTON CROSSES THE DELAWARE RIVER WITH HIS TROOPS. THEY SURPRISE THE BRITISH IN THE BATTLE OF TRENTON IN NEW JERSEY.

OCTOBER 17, 1777

THE PATRIOTS WIN AN IMPORTANT BATTLE AT SARATOGA, NEW YORK.

OCTOBER 1781

THE BRITISH ARMY **SURRENDERS** AT YORKTOWN, VIRGINIA.

GLOSSARY

colony: A piece of land under the control of another country. A person who lives in a colony is a colonist.

defend: To keep something safe.

dependence: The state of being relied on for support.

organize: To be gathered in a group in such a way that it will work well together.

patriot: A person who loves their country.

rebel: Someone who opposes a government. Also, to openly oppose a government.

regiment: A military unit made up of smaller military units.

revolution: A movement to overthrow an established government.

siege: The use of military to surround an area or building in order to capture it.

support: To hold up and help.

surrender: To give up.

traitor: A person who is not faithful to another person or group.

FOR MORE INFORMATION

Books

Murray, Stuart. *American Revolution*. New York, NY: DK Publishing, 2022.

Taylor, Charlotte. *The Truth About Independence Day*. New York, NY: Enslow Publishing, 2023.

Websites

American Revolution

www.dkfindout.com/us/history/american-revolution/
Read even more information about the American Revolution with DK Find Out!

Independence Day

kids.nationalgeographic.com/history/article/independence-day
Discover the causes of the American Revolution in this article for kids.

Publisher's note to educators and parents: Our editors have carefully reviewed these websites to ensure that they are suitable for students. Many websites change frequently, however, and we cannot guarantee that a site's future contents will continue to meet our high standards of quality and educational value. Be advised that students should be closely supervised whenever they access the internet.

INDEX